PRAISE FOR

"Rebecca's work is profoundly and powerfully transformative and is unlike others because hers is rooted in limitless, boundless love. Other teachers want and need identity and that's perfectly fine, but I love that she yields to love over personal identity for your own boundless growth and joy and that of others, and you can quote me on that. I'd have to have daily therapy for 1000 years to uncover and unravel the things I have uncovered and unraveled so quickly while working with Rebecca. Even then, even if I had a thousand years my mind couldn't have seen what my awareness knows. That old sadness is now restored to Love and the clarity that I am whole is restored as well. I love this so much!"

- Kathleen M., Tucson Az.

"My prior 40 years of seeking pale in comparison to the true understanding I have relaxed into after working with Rebecca.

In previous studies, love was mentioned and even emphasized, but was never transmitted in its fullness the way that I have experienced with her."

- B.D., NY

“Rebecca’s work transforms everything for me now. I was intense seeker for truth for last 7 years, but there always was feeling like all this seeking is like job, a constant battle. I tried tons of techniques (I think more than 23 different ones). And this is miraculous! Now I feel tons of love coming out of me and everything just transforms inside of me without doing and everything is just like play. Can't wait to continue in the next series!”

- Dainius, Lithuania

"Rebecca offers the highest truth in the most accessible way. She always keeps things light, easy, and real. While working with her, it feels to me like a bridge is built between my highest understanding and my current perception. This has allowed me to deepen my experience of a peace and love beyond description, while at the same time witnessing changes in my life that I could have previously only wished for. To name just a few: a far greater natural appreciation of myself, smoother and happier relationships, feeling at home in my body and life, and generally living a life that is punctuated by miracles, rather than blanketed by a nondescript "stuckness" that I had felt before working with her."

- L.R.

"I describe Rebecca's work as (truly) integrating the mind, body and spirit. About six weeks in, I said to her "wow, I forgot to worry." My seemingly natural set-point of worry and disapproval was disappearing! Her work is gentle, thoughtful, methodical – and the most profound that I have found."

- Jan, CA

"Rebecca creates such a safe space within which to 'emerge'. She has no judgment. Things that looked to me like 'the end of my world' she was able to put into the perspective of love, and 'poof' it was suddenly a non-issue! I was truly blessed to have had her as a mentor. Thanks Rebecca!"

- Jenny La Fontaine, Intuitive Messenger

More experiences can be found at:
www.RebeccaQuave.com/what-others-say

Remember Who You Are

Reminders from Love

Also by Rebecca Quave:

Allow Love to Be

Remember Who You Are

Reminders from Love

Rebecca Quave

Printed in the United States of America.

You Are Not Broken

You Are What
You Have Been Looking For

Love is All There Is

PREFACE

This book is a collection of reminders from Love.

These reminders each stand on their own, so you can open this book to any page at any time to receive a kernel to integrate.

Take time to absorb the content and allow yourself to curiously explore the space that's being offered.

Let yourself connect with what is alive in the words and more importantly, in the spaces between the words.

All you need is already within you.

This is an opportunity to point your attention back to the changeless Truth within, and rediscover the Love you Are.

Because some of the content is excerpted from live interaction, the tone is sometimes casual and conversational.

Kindly forgive any typographical errors and colloquial expression, and let yourself connect with the underlying Truth as you read.

All nature photos by Rebecca Quave.

All animals were photographed in the wild, undisturbed in their natural habitats.

Special thanks and loving gratitude to Helen Umlah, at www.LoveLightDoodles.com, for offering the inclusion of delightful light codes she received while previewing the contents of this book.

Special thanks and loving gratitude to Katrina Doran, at www.TheWorldofDoranStudio.com, for generously sharing her fountain of lovely ideas and her eye for beauty.

Special thanks and loving gratitude to Vivian Cargille, for creating the love-centered line illustration.

You Are Love and Love is All there is.

Love already loves you more than your mind can try to imitate.

Sunrise near Tortola, BVI

Your strongest yearning is to consciously Be what you Are - to know your oneness with the Love you Are, and rest in that.

The peace which comes from your point of identification residing in Truth is the real happiness, the greatest happiness.

You are here to breathe into expression

all the things Love can Be.

Rose at home

A rose does not burst into bloom by judging the rosebud as wrong.

Are you allowing your life to bloom?

Are you giving space for the Love that you are to express itself through you?

Take a moment in gratitude for all that naturally blooms in you and in your life... allow the Love that you are to bloom fully in and through you.

Love is what supports the blooming of harmony.

Norman Island, near Tortola, BVI

All the worst, most unexplained, most irrational feelings are still the gateways to your deepest Love.

This Love is complete and ever-present.

No experience or feeling can truly eclipse this Love.

Your knowledge of it gives you your longing for it, and that's what makes many feelings seem to feel painful by contrast.

The pain is actually that you are feeling separate from Love, by looking away from Love.

Even in the root of your deepest pain lies your connection with a Love beyond the greatest you can imagine.

Open yourself to all experience.

Allow the fullness of all within you to be embraced.

Feel this Love at the core of everything you encounter.

Be with yourself in this Love.

Experience it with curiosity.

Let your priority become the awareness of this Love in each moment.

What else could be of greater importance?

This is what you are always seeking anyway, so why not embrace it now?

Local park, Miami, Florida

Love provides a peace and a power and a freedom of movement to do what is most helpful in any situation.

You can always experience Love.
You can experience Love in the midst of your mind thinking whatever it thinks.

Offshore from Bimini, Bahamas

Are you in touch with the Loving Joy within you?

Or have you been trying so hard that you've looked right past it?

Joy, not suffering, is your greatest teacher.

Suffering can teach you if you follow it to its source to rediscover the Love that's present.

Let Love bring you deeper to find the continuous current of joy available.

Surrender yourself to what Joy is offering you.

Pay attention to those whispers of infinite Love and amazing possibility. They are reminding you of what you really Are.

Sunset from my patio, Florida

You think you want change, while what you actually crave is the changeless, the Truth.

You look for change because you falsely tie happiness to circumstances.

The current circumstance hasn't fulfilled your longing for happiness, so you think to change it into its opposite will bring happiness.

This cycle can continue on and on, with you manipulating your circumstances by every imaginable means, trying to squeeze happiness from them …

until you seek the changeless Truth you actually crave. Here you can experience the only true happiness.

Pura Tirta Empul, Bali, Indonesia

"Waking up" to Truth is at the same time universal experience and totally unique to you.

It is on one hand universal, but never a "one size fits all" path.

No one has anyone else's answers or instructions for this so-called "path."

One can only be reminded of certain principles that may be helpful in setting themselves on fertile ground for their own particular blooming to unfold.

Bimini, Bahamas

Follow every feeling back to its source.

Allow your existing harmony and perfection to ripple through all of your experience.

Surrender to the truth of Love.

Allow the body to exist within the flood of Love.

Let it be immersed in Love in every moment.

Ubud, Bali, Indonesia

Thank You. I Love You.

Simple as that.

Let your heart overflow with the feelings of "Thank You. I Love You." in each moment, with every breath, toward everything and everyone you encounter...

starting with all of what you think you don't like about yourself or your life.

The true, real Love you are looking for is your very nature.

You cannot be separate from it.

It is all-embracing, all-encompassing, and all-consuming.

It is the fire which engulfs and consumes everything that seems to be its opposite, then burns continually higher and brighter.

Central Park, New York, New York

Be Love.

Be all out.

Let loose the outrageous, all-out Love that you are.

Embrace death, lack, uncertainty - to fully live this experience now.

Be heart-stoppingly alive as an embodiment of infinite Love.

Allow all which springs from that.

Be. Be. Be.

In every moment, be fully, deliciously you.

Offer no impediments to the wellspring of Love which you Are, to the avalanche of abundance which is yours, to the infinite river of life which you are experiencing.

Bali, Indonesia

Would you rather defeat all your enemies, or discover that you have no enemies at all?

Deciding to allow unconditional Love is the only sane thing you can do.

Love is transformative of your fear, your anger, your sadness.

This is because all these emotions were always made of Love.

Bimini, Bahamas

What you've been seeking is what you already Are.

Every experience offers you the gateway to what you seek, if you accept that offer in each moment.

It's only while you rest in what you Are that harmony can shine through.

No amount of manipulation to get the outcome you think you want will ever give you what you are really looking for.

Every misunderstanding, every illusion, is an invitation deeper into Truth.

Sunrise from my balcony, Florida

Your purpose is to know and live the Truth of your-Self.

You won't rest until you live fully in that Truth and experience the Love, Freedom, Peace, and Joy it brings.

Being what you truly are is all you're really looking for.

Knowing yourself as what you truly Are brings the realization of all that is glorious, breathtaking, and lovable beyond measure.

Offshore from Bimini, Bahamas

Live life as a curious exploration of joy.

Living this way will reveal to you the deep Love and Peace which are your very nature.

Let that old sense of heartbreak run to completion. Let it rip through you, cracking everything open, until there is nothing to hide behind.

Let what you held onto (what you thought *was* you) be ripped apart, until you are left standing and shining in all your glory - bare and alive, unhindered and unveiled - no longer hidden behind remnants of misunderstanding, no longer veiled behind expectation, conformity, or apology.

Be that True, unspeakable, immeasurable Love - burning and shining for all.

Rose at home

A fully open, Loving heart cannot be broken. When there is nothing rigid, what can be broken? How do you break an infinite waterfall of pure Love?

If you feel some disappointment, lean into it, experience it fully, give Love the space it needs to remind you of its presence.

When I use the word Love, I don't mean the emotion love, which has an opposite.
I mean Love which has no opposite.
It's an all-embracing, all-encompassing field.

St. Thomas, USVI

Everything you are experiencing is just as sacred as everything that you are looking to experience, that you are hoping to experience, that your mind has gotten the idea is somehow better.

Return your attention to the changeless.

Accept your own Love.

When you embrace the Truth at the core of your very existence, you experience total freedom - no more struggle and nothing to prove.

Disney's Epcot, Walt Disney World, Florida

Your presence allows a reunion with Love.
It seems to be a reunion with love, but nothing was ever separate from Love, it's all made of Love.
When you bring your awareness (your attention, your presence) to something, you withdraw the separations that you put in, and now the Love is free to flow.

Surrender to the Love which even as it is sought after and yearned for, is always there, underneath all the yearning, all the seeking.

Disney's Magic Kingdom, Walt Disney World, Florida

When something looks out of harmony in your life, it's asking for your Love.

You can’t see the Love in something until you are willing to see it exactly as it is.

You already Love yourself infinitely.

Are you ready to receive the Love you Are?

You don't need anything added to you. You don't need anything removed from you.

Bring your point of identification back to the Truth of yourSelf.

Who you Are is unshakeable, and needs nothing added and nothing removed.

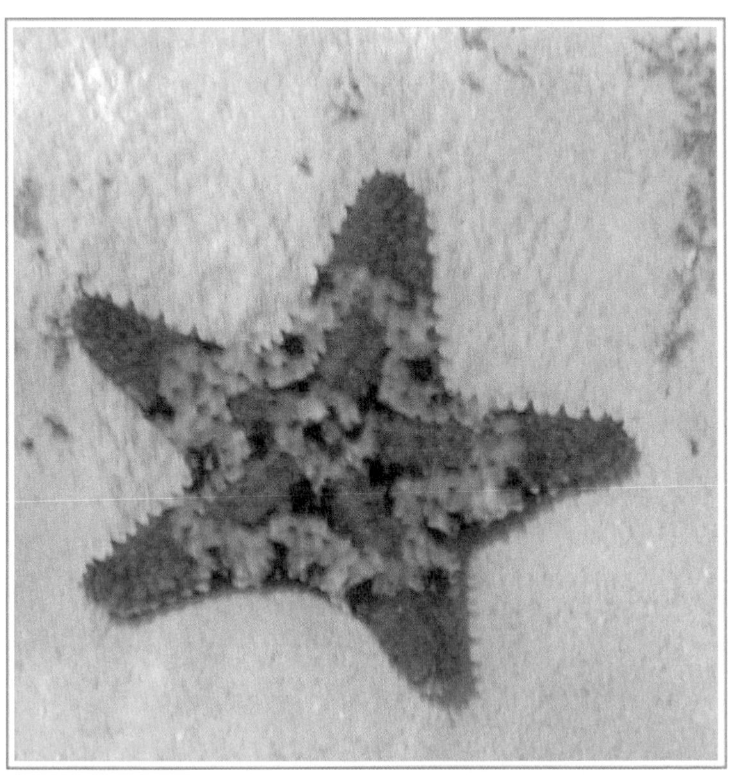

Island near Abaco, Bahamas

All that you think you are, and all that you are striving to be, pales in comparison to the inescapable Truth of your Being.

Are you willing to allow yourself to embody the Truth of what you are?

Your true Being is already more magnificent than anything your mind or ego can try to push you to be or become.

You are already more than what you have been searching for and trying to be.
Are you ready to embrace that?

Candidasa, Bali, Indonesia

Separation is the cause of all suffering.
Rejection is the cause of all experience of separation.

Believing you are separate from Love is your only pain.

Allow your oneness with Love.

Can you step back and give permission for Love to flood through everything, without waiting for your mind to try to generate love, without expecting Love to wait on your ego's opinion of whether or not Love is warranted?

Roses at home

If you can do only one thing, it should be to remember the remarkable gift of Love that you are. Then you would also immediately see how greatly loved, valued, and appreciated you already are.

Rather than struggling to prove yourself in order to get your reward, you would embrace and receive all that is already yours.

You would delight in yourself, your infinite Love and prosperity that comes naturally with being you, and you would happily give the gift of your delight to all - so that they may experience it in themselves.

Offshore from Bimini, Bahamas

The mind often has a misconception that you must choose between Love or action, but there is no either-or.

Love is what gives rise to the most powerful movement or action.

It's not the external movement or stillness that determines the true stillness.

When you tap deep enough into the true stillness, the external can move and move and move, and it makes no difference to your stillness.

When you're not tapped into the true stillness, the external can sit until it rots, and you still won't feel stillness.

Central Park, New York, New York

You feel uncomfortable if you are not aware of your own sovereignty. You feel uncomfortable if you are not aware of your own freedom, and your own choice.

When doing things which feel like 'have to's' or the things which seem automatic, if you recognize the choice you actually do have, and consciously make it, then you'll feel differently about it.

Even doing what you thought you didn't like or thought you were obligated to do, can become joyful when you instead consciously choose to do it.

Ubud, Bali, Indonesia

The ego is simply operating on the terms it understands. The ego works in a structure of matching the information it has to other information. It takes information and extrapolates it in terms of what it already understands.

That's how your spiritual path can seem to get hijacked by the ego, because the ego sits and listens to teachings about having this ever-expanding love, joy and peace, and the only way it knows to understand that or interpret that is, "everything is going to go my way all the time."

So it sets about trying to accomplish that in the way it has accomplished things in the past. The ego thinks it is going to get it, and achieve it, and own it, and finally cross the finish line and finally be enough, get its gold star and have everything go its way all the time.

In reality, everything your ego can conceive of (and more) is already available. The experience of duality plays out over the top of that. So, your ego's understanding is that you have to get from duality playing out to whatever it can conceive of as the true nature of you. However, the True you is always there and the duality is there, superimposed on it. The question is, where is your identification?

Disney's Magic Kingdom, Walt Disney World, Florida

All is already in far greater harmony than you have imagined.

You are blooming beautifully in your inherent magnificence.

Embrace the beauty, joy, and ease, of all opening before you.

You already exist as a self-harmonizing system. Simply allow the Love you Are to move freely and bring all into balance and harmony.

Bimini, Bahamas

When you're identified with the Truth of your Self, you don't have a problem if a feeling of anger shows up in you, or a feeling of sadness, or a feeling of anything.

The more you allow Love to Love everything, the more you allow yourself to experience Love.

Sunrise from my balcony, Florida

All you need to do is not interfere with yourself.

If you stop interfering with your thoughts and feelings by judging them, rejecting them, tinkering with them, trying to improve them, then your attention can rest in Truth.

When you stop interfering in your experience, Love and harmony have the space to prevail.

One of the easiest ways to connect with the Truth of yourSelf, without any preconceived ideas about what it is, without any agenda or expectation, is to connect with what in you has never changed and doesn't ever change.

For every belief or idea you hold strongly, you also perpetuate the opposite belief. Your opposing beliefs create inner tension and conflict which obstructs Truth.

When you disengage from all ideas and beliefs, they all subside and Truth can shine through.

In that space, there is room for Love and Joy to bubble up.

There's been a misunderstanding of the spiritual path that says, "Go get out, up, away to something higher." That's not what it's about.

The Truth is already in you. Its is already what you Are. You're here to be a conduit for it, to let it come all the way through you into full expression here.

Island near Abaco, Bahamas

Loving yourself doesn't mean you do all sorts of shenanigans and gymnastics to force yourself to what you think is the happy end of the scale.

Most people are using self-love as a tool and a manipulation to try to move themselves to one side of duality.

That's never really going to work because it's not what Love is.

What if right where you are, just as you are, without moving an inch or fixing a thing, you are willing to notice the Love already within you, the Love you Are?

Split sky view from my balcony, Florida

Your resistance to feeling certain feelings is all rooted in the belief that any of those feelings can separate you from Love, that you can't experience Love when those feelings are present.
They feel so uncomfortable to you because you reject them.
When you reject them, you are turning away from Love.
You don't allow Love through into your attention in that moment of rejection.

The Truth of you has no reason to resist if any "un-wanted feeling" shows up in its experience any more than the whole sky resists when there's a storm somewhere.

Rose at home

Truth cannot remain hidden. It always reveals itself.
Be curious and give attention to the quiet.
Allow the beauty of Truth to have your full attention.
Give Truth the space to bloom.

Love doesn't mean everything being perfect within duality.
Love means allowing everything to Be.
Love means that it has permission to exist exactly as it Is.
This includes you and all your experiences and your feelings.

Candidasa, Bali, Indonesia

Let Love wash through everything.

Let Love wash through your physical body, through your thoughts, let Love soothe your mind.

Let Love open up the space for all your emotions to move freely and bring themselves back to source and back into harmony.

This lets you return home and lets your point of identification rest back in the Truth of you.
Let Love be the gateway for you.

Local park, Miami, Florida

Enough of "working on it" all.

No more of the parade of new and "greater" spiritual identities to cloak yourself in.

Misunderstanding runs amuck - and becomes most entrenched in those who are "beyond" it, spouting the latest intellectual revelations.

How willing are you to sit with yourself in Love?
With no rules, no labels, no "tradition" or hierarchy to follow?

Would that be too simple?
Do you fear the answers you would find?
(the same ones you claim to endlessly seek)

And it's fine if you do fear it - that's the point.
Are you willing to Love the one who fears?
Rather than fixing, admonishing, or cajoling it into being something "better," something "fearless"?

Are you ready to recognize and accept that the "ego" will never become other than what it is?
Why alternate between decorating it and pushing it on its (self-initiated) pursuit of its own destruction?

Why not Love it all exactly as the imagined creation that it is?

Candidasa, Bali, Indonesia

The most important thing you can do is to remember who and what you really Are.
The knowing of your Self resolves everything else.

Open up to the pure gratitude that is beyond separation, that is not contingent on anything ...
the gratitude that meets everything within you with celebration at its very existence.

Sunrise from my balcony, Florida

You've blamed your mind for seeming to bother you by repeatedly thinking about things. You send it off to solve things, so it tries its best but doesn't have the solution.

Your mind actually brings things in front of your attention because you DO have the solution.

The solution is Love.

Setting everything free to be embraced and harmonized by Love is your decision.

Love without opposite is the true fabric of everything, including you and all of your feelings.

Candidasa, Bali, Indonesia

Connect with what no one can give to you and no one can take away.

Who you Are is unshakeable, already perfect beyond measure, and needs nothing added and nothing removed.

Only the ego/mind is on a quest to remove or destroy the ego/mind.

St. Thomas, USVI

What could be more vital, or more delightful, than a full focus on meeting all with love?
What is more fulfilling than a continuous curiosity for and openness to the truth?
What are you craving for that is not already met by these priorities?
Every motion toward a need to manipulate the external (or internal) is truly a call to go deeper into what is.
There the Truth is revealed. There Love is manifest.

What is so bothersome to you that Truth does not resolve?
Then why expend yourself with struggling, while looking away from Truth?
Turn inward, with innocence and open curiosity. Be fully receptive to all that is available for you.
Allow yourself to be quenched by Truth, refreshed by the light of your being, and nourished in the balm of infinite Love.

There is nowhere you can round up your pain and go put it.
There is nothing outside of you, so there is nowhere to send it.

When you're open, you're open and when you're closed, you're closed.
When you try not to feel a feeling (anger, fear, sadness, etc), then it's also difficult for you to feel the Love that's coursing through your very Being in every moment.
But when you open up, to let yourself feel anything (anger, fear, sadness, etc), now suddenly you can taste the Love too.

Candidasa, Bali, Indonesia

When your identification is placed wholeheartedly in your constructed self, you feel you can be threatened by almost anything.

No one can fix you or save you.
And that's good news because it also means no one can destroy you.

Bangli, Bali, Indonesia

Instead of trying to do anything to a feeling - stop it, change it, manipulate it - just follow it where it goes. Let it take you back to its source.

Everything takes you back to the Truth if you let it.

Love is always present, whether you're aware of it or not.

Offshore from Bimini, Bahamas

Live life as the abundant, magical, infinitely precious being you are.
Treat yourself accordingly by approaching all of life in the knowing that you have set it all out as a gift to yourself.

Put your focus on noticing what in you is changeless.
Let that integrate into your life.
Be that being of Love while doing everything you do.

Sunrise in Bali, Indonesia

Begin at the beginning.
End at the beginning.
The Truth and Love you think you are searching for will steadfastly beckon you from its home as the very essence of you.

No spiritual teacher, no guru, no method or technique or practice, will ever give you what you've really been looking for.
The good news is, you and only you, already have it.

Nusa Penida, Indonesia

The nature of Peace is that there are no outside intrusions to it.
Everything is within you and within that Peace.
Anything which seems to be the opposite of it is just a vehicle to take you deeper into it.

Peace is not "lack of disturbance"
Peace is what you experience when ALL is embraced into the underlying state of perfect Love and Peace
Peace does not mean looking away from, blocking out, or silencing anything
When you reject, silence, and ignore, you may think you feel a temporary "peace," but you've only created more tension of separation
ALL must be acknowledged and embraced for true Love and Peace to prevail
Needing something to quiet down for you to have peace, isn't Peace.

Ubud, Bali, Indonesia

The ego hears of "enlightenment" and uses that to set out on a quest for what it believes is an enrichment of its own worth. It sees enlightenment as the ultimate trophy to acquire.

The further your attention is from Truth, the more you feel there is to lose; the more you feel your identity is at stake.

When you have no preconceived expectation or agenda, you are free to discover all Truth.

Sunset from my patio, Florida

Who do you think you are?
No matter what it is, you are more than that.
If you can think it, it's not the Truth of you.

What you Are can only be perceived, felt directly. And when you do, you'll find that it outshines anything you ever could've hoped for.

The body and mind on their own cannot feel free and unlimited. They are by design, finite.
What you *can* feel is allowing your unlimited nature to flow through them.
Then they can relax and cooperate with your expression. They can be in service to, and fully supported by all you Are.

Candidasa, Bali, Indonesia

What is the truth of any problem?
What disturbs you?
And how is it resolved?
What is the one solution you require?
When you encounter what you consider a problem, what really disturbs you?
You resist your own experience, you reject your own feelings.
You fear the worst, and the worst is just what you don't want to feel.

But what if you allow yourself to feel it all?
What if you offer a Loving embrace to it all?
What can harm you then?

Offshore from Bimini, Bahamas

Every breath offers you a choice between Truth and illusion.

Your difficulty is in clinging to certain identities, reaching for certain identities, rejecting certain identities, all with the sense that those identities are what is real.

What liberates you, is a recognition of what you truly Are, so the comings and goings of any of those identities becomes insignificant to you.

What your mind calls a miracle, your true Being calls standard operating procedure.

Go in Grace.
Wherever you are, whatever you seem to be doing, allow your Being to lead the way.
All you are ever really doing anyway is conducting Love.
Radiate Love and Truth - that is your occupation.
Where there seem to be problems, move deeper into Truth, open fully to Love.
Remain surrendered to Love; yield to it.
Let Love live through you.

Offshore from Bimini, Bahamas

Stop asking the mind to "do" unconditional Love.
You ARE it.

Transformation is created by diving deep into the center of something to find out what is actually there.
Then allow that to take over.
A caterpillar is already perfect and already contains the butterfly.

Goa Gajah, Bali, Indonesia

It's not what's happening, but who you think you are while it is happening, that determines your experience.

Any suffering you've ever experienced was because your point of identification was not resting in Truth.

Ubud, Bali, Indonesia

Leave behind the misunderstanding of separation between what you call mundane and what you call profound; between what you call material and what you call spiritual. There is no difference.

Stop holding yourself in what you thought you were.

Pura Mengening, Bali, Indonesia

When you stay present with your direct experience, you immediately have access to what you already Are (which is Love).

It just comes rushing through where you thought it wasn't there. That imaginary, imposed separation falls and everything harmonizes.

Island near Abaco, Bahamas

Unlimited means you have the freedom to experience everything within you. You give yourself permission for everything. Everything.

There's nothing that's not embraced by Love, and nothing can disturb what is changeless.

The answer to everything is Truth, and Truth is changeless.

Goa Gajah, Bali, Indonesia

Be fully yourSelf and let it shine through the stained glass kaleidoscope of your costume, your assumed identity.

Let yourself be in expression of _____ instead of in pursuit of ______.

A perfectly polished and maintained acorn pales in comparison to the vibrantly alive and expanding oak tree that it could be when it is willing to go underground in the dark and split wide open.

Sunset in Ubud, Bali, Indonesia

Your suffering stems from not recognizing the changeless which contains the ever-changing.

All along, your experience was never the problem, your rejection of it was.
What matters is not what happens in your experience, but who you think you are while it's happening.

Sunset in Bimini, Bahamas

Offer Love in each moment ...
remembering that there is only Now and there is only Love.

Ask yourself:
What do I want to avoid experiencing?
What do I think it means about me?
What is the Truth of this?

Sunset from my patio, Florida

What if what you Are is something other than anything you ever thought you were?

You Are Love and Love is All there is.

Remember, there is no finish line

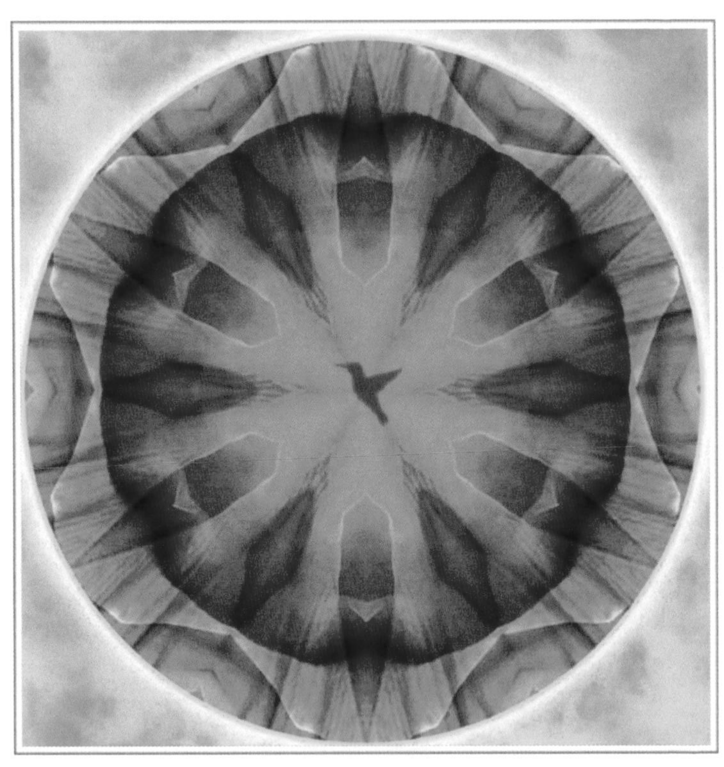

ABOUT REBECCA QUAVE

Rebecca is a catalyst of transformation and expansion of consciousness. She guides and supports you in unraveling exactly what's in the way of embodying and expressing the expansive love and unlimited potential you truly are. Her natural gift of activating you to your highest truth creates profound shifts quickly and easily.
Because of her loving and surrendered nature which embraces you and your personal journey exactly as you are while supporting and guiding your unique process, some describe Rebecca as a midwife of spiritual expansion and embodiment.

You can visit Rebecca at www.RebeccaQuave.com

Other books by Rebecca are available at
www.RebeccaQuave.com/books

Receive updates and inspiration by signing up at
www.RebeccaQuave.com/email

Made in the USA
Middletown, DE
09 October 2020

21448181R00075